Taste and Smell describes the remarkable way in which our senses of taste and smell work together to give us information about our surroundings. How we are able to taste and smell is explained, and different types of tastes and smells, both past and present, are discussed. Children are encouraged to explore their senses of taste and smell by simple, safe experiments. The uses of taste and smell, by people, animals and insects, are also examined.

© Macdonald & Co. (Publishers) Ltd. 1985
First published in Great Britain in 1985
by Macdonald & Co. (Publishers) Ltd.
London & Sydney

Adapted and published in the
United States in 1987 by
Silver Burdett Company
Morristown, N.J.

Library of Congress Cataloging-in-Publication Data

Allen, John.
    Taste and smell.

    (Let's look up)
    Bibliography: p.
    Includes index.
    Summary: Text and illustrations describe the senses of taste and smell,
how they function, and their importance in our daily life.
    1. Chemical senses—Juvenile literature. 2. Taste—Juvenile literature.
3. Smell—Juvenile literature. [1. Taste. 2. Smell. 3. Senses and sensation]
I. Title.
QP455.A35 1987   612'-86   86-6658
ISBN 0-382-09175-2

TASTE
AND SMELL

John Allen

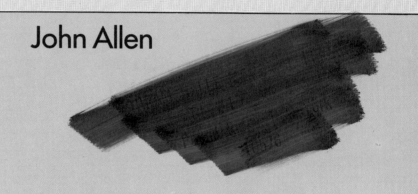

DANGER!

**Never taste or smell any unknown
substances. They could be dangerous.**

**Silver Burdett Company
Morristown, New Jersey**

How to use this book

First, look at the contents page opposite. Read the chapter list to see if it includes the subject you want. The list tells you what each page is about. You can then find the page with the information you need.

If you want to know about one particular thing, look it up in the index on page 31. For example, if you want to know about taste buds, the index tells you that there is something about them on page 12. The index also lists the pictures in the book.

When you read this book, you will find some unusual words. The glossary on page 30 explains what they mean.

Series Editor
Margaret Conroy

Book Editor
Fiona Macdonald

Production
Susan Mead

Picture Research
Suzanne Williams

Factual Adviser
Geoff Watts

Reading Consultant
Amy Gibbs
Inner London Education Authority
Centre for Language in Primary
Education

Series Design
Robert Mathias/Anne Isseyegh

Book Design
Jane Robison

Teacher Panel
Lena Andrew,
Brian Haigh

Illustrations
Dave Eaton Front Cover
Catherine Bradbury Pages 6, 9, 25, 26-27
Ginny Maddison Page 15
Kevin Maddison Pages 8, 10, 12, 13, 14-15, 21, 28-29
Kate Rogers Pages 7, 16, 18-19

Photographs
Barnaby's Picture Library 14-15
BPCC/Aldus Archive 17, 20-21T
Sally and Richard Greenhill 10-11
OSF/JAL Cooke 23B
REGA, Swiss Air-Ambulance 26
Seaphot/Jorge Provenza 24
Survival Anglia/Cindy Buxton 23T
ZEFA cover photographs, 18, 20B

CONTENTS

TASTING AND SMELLING

How we taste and smell

This book is about taste and smell. Taste and smell are two of our five senses. The others are sight, hearing and touch. All our senses work together to tell us about the world.

In people, the sense of sight is probably the most useful and important. But many animals use their senses of taste and smell far more than their sense of sight. They rely on smells to carry messages or to warn of approaching danger. They rely on taste to tell them whether something is safe to eat. Most animals have a much better sense of taste and smell than humans. Dogs can smell a million times better!

Moles live underground where it is very dark. They use their sense of smell to find food.

Think how dull and strange it would be if you were not able to taste your favorite foods and drinks. Without your sense of taste, you would find it hard to tell the difference between a sweet cookie and a salty cheese cracker without looking. And think how odd it would be to sniff an onion, or a rose, and find that they smelled of nothing at all. Without your sense of smell, you could not enjoy the perfume of spring flowers or the smell of your supper cooking!

We get some idea of what it might be like to lose our senses of taste and smell when we catch a bad cold. Fortunately, they quickly return to us as soon as we get better.

We enjoy our food more if it tastes and smells good! How many different tastes and smells can you see in this picture?

Noses

Humans use their noses to draw in smells floating in the air. Other animals have different ways of collecting smells. Snakes use their tongues, catfish use their whiskers and moths use their antennae, or feelers. Sea anemones trap smells with their waving tentacles. The kiwi has nostrils which breathe in smells right at the tip of its long beak.

If you could see inside your nose it would look rather like this. Smells are recognized by special cells at the back of the nose.

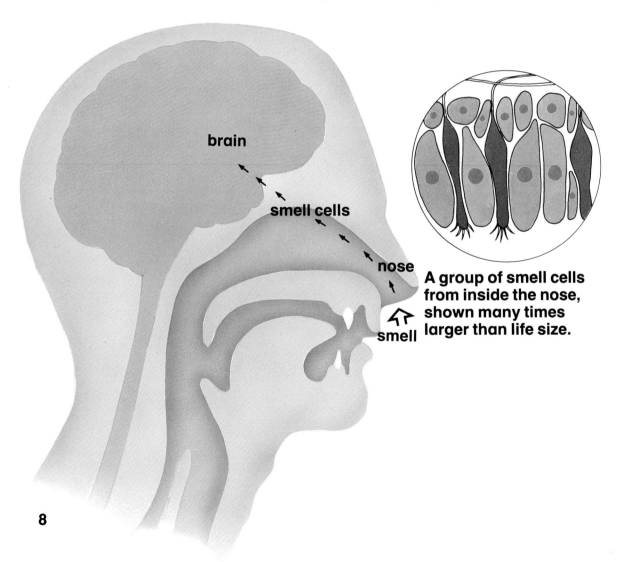

brain

smell cells

nose

smell

A group of smell cells from inside the nose, shown many times larger than life size.

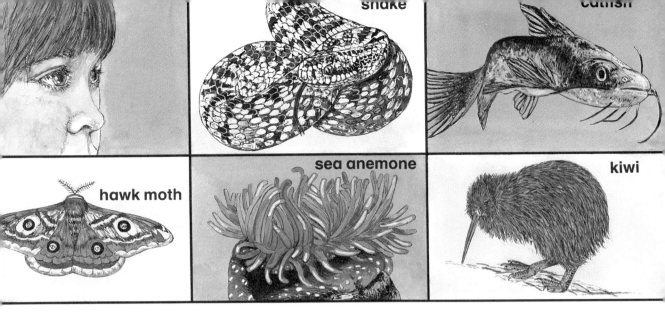

snake

catfish

sea anemone

kiwi

hawk moth

There are many different ways of smelling. Each of these drawings shows a different way of collecting the smells that float in air or water.

In humans, noses come in many different shapes and sizes. But whatever their shape, noses all have the same job to do. They help us to breathe and they help us to smell.

The nose helps us to breathe by acting as a filter. The hairs in the nostrils stop insects and large pieces of dust from getting into the lungs. The damp lining of the nose sends a stream of sticky liquid down the back of the nose and throat. This sticky liquid is called mucus and it traps any dirt and germs that are in the air. The nose also warms cold air as it is breathed in from outside the body.

There are some special cells at the back of the nose which help us to smell. They are covered with tiny hairs and are usually wet, because they are covered with mucus. As air is breathed in through the nose, these smell cells trap any smelly substances it contains and then send messages about them to the brain.

How smell works

See how many foods or drinks you can identify by smell alone. Ask a friend to blindfold you and then to offer you some different foods or drinks to smell. Try smelling tea, coffee, milk, fruit juice, and water.

We can only smell something if it gives off a vapor. Things give off vapor in the same way that boiling water gives off steam, except that usually we cannot see the vapor. The vapor mixes with the air and enters our noses when we breathe in. Some of the vapor lands on special smell cells at the back of the nose. The cells send a message to the brain to tell us that there is a smell in the air.

Objects such as glass, stone and metal do not usually give off any vapor. Therefore we cannot smell them. Some liquids, such as gasoline or perfume, give off vapor very easily. We can sometimes smell them from quite far away.

Many animals have an excellent sense of smell. Pigs can identify food buried underground by using their sense of smell.

Our noses can often detect very faint traces of a smell. If it is an unpleasant smell, such as rotten eggs, we soon wrinkle our noses and hold our breath. This stops any of the smelly vapor from entering our noses. If the smell is a pleasant one, like food or flowers, then we often take a deep breath or breathe in slowly. This lets more of the smelly vapor enter our noses and we can enjoy the smell for longer.

We quickly get used to any smell, whether it is pleasant or unpleasant. The smell seems to fade and we are no longer aware of it. It is as if our sense of smell becomes tired. Test this for yourself by smelling an orange or a lemon.

How taste works

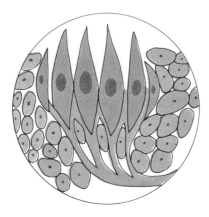

A taste bud, shown many times life size.

Your tongue helps you to speak clearly. It also helps you to taste your food. If you look in a mirror and stick your tongue out, you will see many tiny bumps on its surface. These bumps are called taste buds. Each one contains up to 20 taste cells. Altogether there are about 5,000 taste buds and nearly 100,000 taste cells on your tongue.

The taste buds are arranged in four main groups on the tongue. Each group can detect a certain kind of taste. The four main tastes are sweet, bitter, salt and sour. Once the taste buds have recognized a particular taste in our food, they pass messages on to our brains.

There are four groups of taste buds on the tongue. Each group identifies one of the four main tastes – salt, sweet, sour, bitter. Salty tastes are recognized by taste buds at the tip of the tongue, sweet and sour tastes by those at the sides, and bitter tastes by taste buds at the back of the tongue.

As we chew our food, we produce a watery liquid in our mouths. This is saliva, which helps us to swallow our food. It also helps our taste buds to identify what we are eating because they cannot detect any tastes in food unless the food is mixed with water. Saliva dissolves dry food, such as biscuits, in our mouths and then the taste buds can identify it. Substances that will not dissolve in water, such as glass or stone, seem tasteless. This is because the taste buds cannot find out about them.

Our senses of taste and smell work very closely together. Sometimes the sense of smell can trick the tastebuds, as the experiment on this page shows. When we take nasty medicine, we hold our noses. This means that our brains get messages from our tastebuds alone.

Taste and smell work closely together, but the sense of smell is more powerful. Try this experiment and see how your sense of smell can confuse your sense of taste. Ask a friend to hold a piece of raw onion under your nose. At the same time, ask your friend to give you a piece of cold cooked potato or bread to eat. You will find that the bread or potato tastes of onion, even though you are not eating any onion!

TASTES AND SMELLS

Smells all around us

We can often tell where we are just by using our sense of smell. If you go out for a walk, you will notice that different places have their own distinct smell. We can easily tell when we are approaching a fish market, a hot-dog stand or a bakery. In a park or garden, you may find a different set of smells, but these will depend on the time of year. In the autumn, you might smell bonfires. In the summer, there will be the scent of flowers and perhaps the smell of newly-mown grass. In industrial towns, some factories give off unpleasant smells. On busy streets or highways, you can be sure to find the smell of traffic exhaust fumes.

You can find lots of different smells indoors, too. Can you make a list of the smells found in your home or school? The kitchen will have a delicious smell of cooking food at mealtimes. The bathroom or cloakrooms may smell strongly of soap or disinfectant. We usually take all these smells for granted, but life would be very dull without them.

Smells can also remind us of places we have visited in the past. A damp, musty smell might remind you of a trip to an old house, or the smell of flowers bring back a walk in the country.

Many stores have an easily recognizable smell, like this fish store.

cooking smells

drains

compost

14

smoke

Bakers

Park

Lorry

Factory

food

flowers

grass

You can make a smell map of your house or of the streets around your house or school. Mark the smells you find around you on your own drawings. Ask a friend or two to follow the map. Do they find the same smells?

15

Tastes in food and drink

We all enjoy the taste of our favorite foods and drinks. Some foods taste good when they are raw. Others need cooking before we can eat them. Sometimes extra ingredients are added while food is being cooked to improve its taste.

Herbs and spices make food taste pleasant. They come from the leaves, roots and seeds of certain plants. Today, we use herbs and spices to improve the taste of food, but in the past they were often used to help preserve meat and fish.

A kitchen in the past would have been full of strong tastes and smells from herbs and spices used in cooking, and from salted and pickled foods.

Hundreds of years ago, people did not have refrigerators or canned and frozen food. Meat and fish were stored for the winter in barrels of salt or vinegar, or were dried and smoked. Herbs and spices covered up the flavor of preserved food that was beginning to go bad. Their strong flavors went well with the sour or salty tastes of the preserved food. The most commonly used herbs were sage, rosemary and thyme. Spices such as pepper, ginger, nutmeg and cloves were also popular.

Many spices grow only in countries where there is a hot climate. But herbs will grow in most gardens or in a pot on a sunny windowsill. Try sowing seeds of parsley, chives, chervil and coriander. You can also buy a wide range of dried herbs and spices in shops. Try to find out what herbs and spices are used in your meals.

A wonderful collection of spices! Most of them are ground into fine powder, ready to use in cooking. But you can clearly identify some – long black vanilla pods, dried root ginger, whole nutmegs and lacy orange "blades" of mace.

Smells in the past

Everybody has their own particular smell, even when they are washed and clean. You will not notice your own smell because it is with you all the time. But if you have a pet dog or cat it will probably recognize you by using its sense of smell rather than its eyesight.

Nowadays, we are encouraged to use scented soaps and perfumes to cover up our natural smell, and to smell pleasant all the time. But in the past, people were not always as clean as most of us are today. They threw their rubbish and dirty water out into the streets. Wealthy people used perfume to try and disguise some of the nasty smells around them.

The ancient Chinese burned sweet-smelling incense when they prayed to their gods.

Gathering rose petals to make into perfume. Several tons of petals are needed to make one small bottle of rose essence.

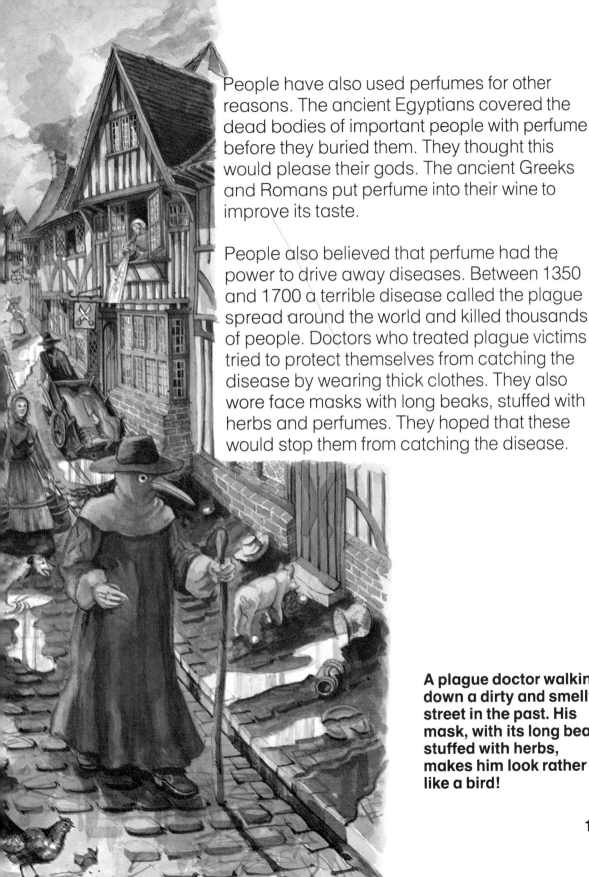

People have also used perfumes for other reasons. The ancient Egyptians covered the dead bodies of important people with perfume before they buried them. They thought this would please their gods. The ancient Greeks and Romans put perfume into their wine to improve its taste.

People also believed that perfume had the power to drive away diseases. Between 1350 and 1700 a terrible disease called the plague spread around the world and killed thousands of people. Doctors who treated plague victims tried to protect themselves from catching the disease by wearing thick clothes. They also wore face masks with long beaks, stuffed with herbs and perfumes. They hoped that these would stop them from catching the disease.

A plague doctor walking down a dirty and smelly street in the past. His mask, with its long beak stuffed with herbs, makes him look rather like a bird!

Modern day smells

Herbs, spices and other scents are still used today to make our surroundings more pleasant. We no longer need perfumes to cover the dreadful smells in our streets, but people still wear perfumes when they want to smell nice.

Perfumes are made from a variety of ingredients. They are blended by very skilled people, called perfumiers. Perfumiers have an excellent sense of smell and are trained to recognize thousands of different scents. Many of the ingredients of perfumes have not changed for hundreds of years. The flowers and leaves of plants are still used, and also certain chemicals taken from animals.

A perfumier makes perfume by blending many different smells together. He uses the long strips of paper to test the mixture of smells.

Today, many different types of perfumes and cosmetics are sold in shops.

The chemicals taken from animals, especially whales, deer and beavers, make a perfume last longer. However, many people today do not like to think that animal products have been used for a luxury such as perfume that we do not really need. They think it is cruel to use animals in this way.

Many perfumes are now made in laboratories, from chemicals which copy the smells found in animals and plants. Perfumes made in this way are much cheaper than perfumes made from flowers and animal products. They are used in everyday items such as soap, washing powder and furniture polish, as well as in the perfumes we wear. You could even make your own perfumes. Try a scented pomander, or an orange studded with cloves.

| **Collect scented flowers** | **Remove petals** | **Dry in a warm place** |
| **Make a bag this way** | **Add dried petals** | **Your pomander is ready** |

USES OF TASTE AND SMELL

Tastes and smells that attract

We all have a favorite food that we like to eat. There are several reasons why we might enjoy it. It could depend on a liking for one of the four main tastes – sweet, salt, sour, bitter. It could depend on what food is available where you live, since such a variety of food is found throughout the world. Or it could depend on the sort of food you are used to eating. Some people like to try new and different tastes. Others prefer to keep to what they know.

Sharks are attracted to their prey by the smell of blood.

Baby fur seals recognize their mothers by using their sense of smell.

Animals also have their favorite foods. Animals' tastes have developed over millions of years so that they usually choose to eat food that is good for them.

Animals also have preferences for certain smells. They often use their sense of smell to lead them to a food supply. Peacock butterflies are attracted to the smell of nettles. They travel long distances to lay their eggs on nettle leaves. In this way, their caterpillars will be sure of a suitable food supply close at hand when they hatch from the eggs.

Using its sense of smell, this butterfly has chosen to lay its eggs on a cabbage plant.

23

Tastes and smells that repel

If food is left unwrapped for a long time in a warm place it will begin to go bad and smell unpleasant. Tiny living things, called bacteria, cause the smell as they make the food rot. Some of these bacteria can harm us and cause diseases. We have learned that a bad smell sometimes means bad food, which will make us ill, but many animals do not seem to be affected by eating rotten food. Rats and seagulls can often be seen around smelly rubbish heaps and trash cans. Other animals for example, cats, are more choosy.

Skunks spray a nasty-smelling liquid from glands near their tails to drive away their attackers.

Some plants taste very bitter. This stops them from being eaten by people and animals. If you put something that is bitter into your mouth, you will probably spit it out! Some animals can protect themselves in the same ways as these plants. They produce bitter or nasty-smelling liquids as a warning to other animals to keep away.

Humans have learned from animals and plants how to put bad smells to good uses. We make nasty-smelling chemicals to keep away unwanted pests, such as clothes moths. Deep-sea divers sometimes carry special shark-repellent sprays with them for safety. These spray a strong-smelling liquid into the sea which hides the scent of the human from the shark. It also drives any nearby sharks away because they do not like the smell!

Toads produce a bitter-tasting slime to cover their skins when they are attacked. Dogs soon learn not to pick them up in their mouths!

Messages sent by smell

Although our sense of smell is useful to us, we use it very little when compared with many animals. They send and receive many different messages by smell. Animals and insects send smell messages by producing special chemicals from various parts of their bodies. These chemicals are called pheromones.

Ants leave a smell trail for others to follow.

Dogs are well known for their habit of marking their territory by urinating against trees and posts. Cats rub their faces against their owner's legs to mark the humans as their property.

Animals' sense of smell can be used to help people. This dog works with a mountain rescue team to find climbers buried in the snow.

When animals are looking for a mate, they will often use smell to attract each other. This is particularly important for some rare animals and insects, who may have to travel far to find a partner. The female's smell is carried on the breeze over a large area, and will eventually lead a likely partner to her.

People use animals that have a good sense of smell to help them. Dogs can be trained to find people who are lost in swamps or on mountains. Even the slight traces of scent given off by someone's shoes are enough for many dogs to follow. Other dogs are trained to help save lives by sniffing out explosives and drugs.

The musk deer marks its territory by leaving its scent on trees. It produces the scent from a special gland near its tail.

FINDING OUT MORE

Experiments

How sensitive is your sense of taste? This experiment will help you to find out. Find five cups, and fill them about a quarter full with fresh water. Now put one drop of peppermint food flavoring essence into the first cup, two drops into the second cup, three drops into the third cup and four drops into the fourth cup. Do not put any flavoring into the fifth cup. Label each cup to show how many drops you used. Now ask your friends to blindfold you while they mix up the order of the cups. Now, still blindfolded, try to arrange the cups in the correct order, ranging from the strongest tasting peppermint flavor to plain water. Did you get the order right?

For this experiment you will need five cups, some water and some peppermint food flavoring essence. A medicine dropper, or a teaspoon, and some sticky labels would also be useful. You will also need a friend or two to help you.

How far do some smells travel? This experiment will help you to find out. One person should be blindfolded in the middle of a big room, or in the open air. The second person should walk slowly towards them, carrying a smelly substance. When the blindfolded person first smells the substance, they should call out, and the person carrying the substance should stand still. The people who are helping to measure distances should measure how far it is between the blindfolded person and the one carrying the smelly substance and record it on a chart. You will find that some substances can be smelled from much farther away than others.

For this experiment, you will need four people, one to sit blindfolded, one to carry smelly substances, and two to measure and record distances. You will also need a measuring tape, pencils and paper, and lots of smelly substances to test!

DANGER!

Never taste or smell any unknown substances. They could be dangerous.

GLOSSARY, BOOKS TO READ

A glossary is a word list. This one explains unusual words that are used in this book.

Bacteria Tiny living things found all around us. Some of them can cause illness.

Cell A tiny part of your body. Your whole body is made up of millions and millions of tiny cells.

Disease Another word for an illness.

Germs A word used to describe all kinds of minute living things, including bacteria, which can cause illness.

Herbs Leaves of plants with a pleasant taste or smell that are used to make food taste good. They can be fresh or dried.

Mucus The sticky liquid produced inside the nose. It helps to trap germs and dust.

Nostrils The holes at the end of our nose through which we breathe.

Perfumier A person with a very good sense of smell who makes perfumes by mixing different-smelling substances together.

Pheromones Special smelly chemicals produced by insects to attract a mate.

Plague An illness which killed many people in the past. It was caused by a type of bacteria.

Saliva The liquid produced in our mouths. It helps us to taste our food by dissolving dry substances in water.

Senses The five ways in which people find out about the world around them. The five different senses are: sight, hearing, touch, taste and smell.

Spices The dried bark, seeds or roots of certain plants which have a pleasant taste and smell. Like herbs, they are used to flavor food.

Taste buds Groups of special cells on our tongues. They enable us to recognize different tastes in the food we eat. The four main tastes are salt, sour, sweet and bitter.

Tentacles The waving "arms and legs" of the sea creatures like octopuses and sea anemones.

Vapor Minute particles of a substance floating in the air. For example, steam is water vapor.

BOOKS TO READ

You can find out more about taste and smell in these books.

BOOKS TO READ
Taste, Touch and Smell by Irving Adler and Ruth Adler, Harper and Row, 1966.
Taste and Smell, Ed Catherall, Silver Burdett, 1982.
Five Senses by Keith Brandt, Troll Associates, 1985.
Tasha Tudor's Five Senses by Tasha Tudor, Platt and Munk, 1978.
Touch, Taste and Smell by Brian Ward, Franklin Watts, 1982.
How do we Smell? by Pat Blakely, Creative Education, 1982.
Smells: Things to do with Them by D. Gribble and H. McPhee, Penguin Books, 1978.

INDEX

The **dark** numbers tell you where you will find a picture of the subject